YOU ARE A LYRICAL GENIUS!!!

A Simple New Approach To

Writing Great & Honest Lyrics

by chazaray

for those about to rock

EVERYONE can write great lyrics!!!

I used to not think so. BUT NOW I DO!!! Maybe none of us are destined to write like Mick Jagger, but we can still do it.

Think about it. There are country lyricists, rock lyricists, hip-hop lyricists, pop lyricists, jazz lyricists, etc, etc, etc... BUT!!! Do think Jay-Z can write a great country song? Do you think David Bowie can write a great rap song? Probably not. (Okay, maybe they could but you get my point.) There are all sorts of lyrical styles and genres out there so to say that you can either write lyrics or you can't is a totally flawed statement. You CAN write great lyrics!! You just have to find out what kind of lyricist you are.

READ ON!!!

I just looked at the best-selling lyric writing books. There are a few that seem really popular, written by well-educated scholarly types who have an insanely in-depth perspective on songwriting. Their books are 200+ pages and probably have heaps and heaps of useful info... BUT!!! It's tough for me to comprehend most of that stuff and I'm not sure I could get through the whole thing and do all the recommended drills and exercises. This might work for some folks, just not my folks. If something can't be explained in simple terms then it's going to be difficult for me to understand. That's just me. I was never much of a student. As a lifelong struggling songwriter, I know I would read almost ANYTHING that could help, and if I could get through and understand a 200 page book I probably would.

SO!!!

This book is not all that!!! It's NOT some long-winded academic exercise. It's NOT some intense exploration into musical theory. This book is simple and to the point AND it's only 30 pages.

BUT!!!

I believe the next 30 pages will change your songwriting life IMMEDIATELY... and forever.

WHY???

Because 30 pages are all you need!!!

REALLY!!!

I mean, over-thinking was my biggest problem with lyric writing. What about you??? So this book is not about that!!! In 30 pages, I share a simple approach to lyric and songwriting that I learned on my own that has completely changed the way I write. There's no over-thinking, over-studying, over-the-top exercises, overly-complex language, etc. etc. etc. Everyone can understand it and anyone can do it. Heck, if you can't then get a refund. Simple as that.

AND!!!

No words will be wasted describing what a song is or isn't and getting deep into the meaning of life and all that. I don't know about you, but that's never helped me write a song. It's only confused me (more so than I already was) and given me false confidence that never yielded results.

A lot of books mention the need to establish an emotional connection with your audience and the need to write universal lyrics. You know what??? Don't ever think about doing that!!! That's the complete opposite approach you should take. There were exactly 3 hit songs written solely to connect with an audience without the writers feeling the feelings themselves and all 3 of those songs were written in the 1970's. So forget it.

Later in this book I'll show you how, but if you write from your heart - if you write with HONESTY - then your song *will* be a hit (at least for yourself), and if others connect with it so be it. You can't spend your life 'trying' to connect. I mean, I suppose you could, but why bother???

An audience will connect with honesty. That's the bottom line. They won't connect with forced words, fake attitudes, cultivated nonsense AND they can detect a fraud quickly!!! So pay no mind to the *'you need to connect'* gibberish. This book is about staying true to yourself and letting the chips fall where they may. If you're not honest, then your song has no chance. Guaranteed.

I'd also like to add that I don't believe you can write a 'hit' song after reading a book. Anyone who says otherwise is just trying to sell you something. Hit songs happen at random and writing hit songs is not what this book is about.

This book is about writing great songs for yourself - because you've spent countless hours trying to do so without success. This book will show you a very simple method on how to write songs that will be your own 'hit.' (Now, if one of your songs became a mainstream commercial 'hit,' then well... that'd be good news! And it's certainly possible.) This book is ONLY about writing great respectable lyrics and songs without any over-thinking, and learning how to do it quickly. It'll only take you moments to read but could change your songwriting life forever.

OK???

SO LET'S GET STARTED!!!!!!

About me: I mostly wrote alternative rock songs, but it was literally impossible for me to write lyrics. IMPOSSIBLE!!! I'd pull my hair out and get dizzy trying to think of them and they just never came. Finally, I would give up and sloppily finish the song and all the lyrics would make no sense and most of it was trash. Sure, there'd be some good lines here and there, but as a whole the song would suck and it wasn't honest and no one, including myself, liked it. To this day, I can't listen to my old songs and it's only because of crappy, stupid, forced, illogical, lame lyrics.

But then…

After years and years of this torture…

I finally had a breakthrough!!! And I want to share this with EVERYONE who's ever pulled out their hair trying to write good lyrics.

Like I mentioned, you might not be the next Mick Jagger... BUT!!! You'll be able to write something respectable that others will appreciate and say, yeah, that's cool. 30 years from now you can play it without shame for your family, friends, and most importantly, for yourself.

In the beginning, this lyric writing method might require you to tinker with your chosen genre of music. It can still be rock, country, hip-hop, or whatever, but you'll have to change it up a bit at first. This will make sense soon, just keep reading.

BUT FIRST!!!

Let's go over some songwriting basics which you probably already know, but if not, you really should:

1. KEEP TENSE CONSISTENT:
GOOD
*I **went** to a bar*
*And **drank** from a jar*

BAD
*I **went** to a bar*
*And **drink** from a jar*

2. KEEP PRONOUNS CONSISTENT
GOOD
***She** is awesome and sweet*
*I love **her** big hair and I love **her** big feet*

BAD
***She** is awesome and sweet*
*I love **your** big hair and I love **your** big feet*

3. RHYMES NEED NOT BE EXACT
Don't get stuck on exact rhymes. Something like the following works great:

*I walked along the **river***
*Dirt poor but somehow **richer***

OK!!!

That's it for basics rules. I recommend sticking to them when you're starting out.

SO HERE WE GO!!!!!!!!!!!!!!!

Are you ready to change your songwriting life forever???

WAIT!!!

ONE LAST THING!!!

Let me make one thing clear: If you have a pile of incomplete songs with lyrical ideas; if you have most of the melodies done and most of the vowel sounds worked out (Ugh!!! Sound familiar???), then stash ALL these songs away. You won't need them. You can come back to them later but you have to move on and try what I'm about to show you. Why??? Well, the old way ain't working out so well, now is it? I have a stash of my own incomplete songs. Every one of them has melodies and vowel sounds, but none of them have any legitimate lyrics. These songs are dead ends.

Until you find yourself as a writer and boost your lyric writing confidence, you have to put these songs on hold. You can come back to them later, but not now. You have to start from scratch and I'm going to show you how.

BUT!!!

DON'T!!!

WORRY!!!

The whole process you're about to learn can take you as little as one night!!! So put your old material away and focus on the lesson at hand. Okay???

OK!!!!!

Let's get STARTED!!!

It's important for you to move at your own pace and work in a way most comfortable to you. You can get the following done in one night, or one week, or whenever, but I suggest you taking your time and doing it all and doing it right. Just follow the method as it's written and try not to jump ahead. I'm not the most patient person in the world so I know the urge to move quickly and skip things, but you'll probably be better off if you don't. Now…

ARE YOU READY???

OK!!!!!

Here's the FIRST step:

1. Whatever your instrument is, write a progression with any two chords that sound good to you. Maybe G to C, or Am to Em, or D to A. Whatever you want. Make them abstract if you want. It doesn't matter.

2. Play them and keep playing them.

3. Soon you'll start to hear a possible melody. (Sounds familiar, right???)

BUT WAIT!!!!

Here's what I want you to do:

4. Come up with ONE WORD!!! (That's right!!! Just one word!!!)

5. Sing that one word until you have a good melody for it (either the melody you heard or something new).

6. When you got that down, add a 3rd chord to give the progression more dynamics... BUT!!! Make sure you keep the original two chord progression dominant. Just add the 3rd chord when the song

needs it.

7. Make sure the one word you think of is from your heart. BE HONEST!!! What ONE WORD describes you? What one word describes the way you feel right now? What one word sums up your life? What one word makes you smile? What one word do you dream about being?

8. Record the song (or keep playing it), add cool sounds, instrumental melodies, solo's, textures - whatever you need to make it interesting. Shave the song down to a few minutes, use the singing sparingly, and...

BOOM!!!!!

You just wrote a great song with amazing lyrics!!!

Okay, maybe more like a great song with a *single* 'lyric.'

BUT THAT'S HOW YOU START!!!!!

THAT'S THE FIRST STEP!!!!

CAN YOU DIG IT?!?!?

You're essentially writing a instrumental (with as much instrumental melody as you like) and you're adding one word to bring it all together. It's an awesome way to start learning how to write great and honest lyrics.

SO!!!

Throw out everything you know - all your old conventions, all those hopeless little poems, all those verse/verse/chorus disasters - and try this out!!!

NOW!!!

Check out my website (www.chazaray.com) - powered by the cool and awesome BandCamp.com (which I highly recommend to everyone) - and listen to BREAKDOWN. This is the first song I wrote using this method. The singing doesn't come in until the end of the song, but that's ok. This was experimental and I felt the end was the best place for it. The one word I sing is:

Breakdown

This is a very honest lyric for me because '*Breakdown*' is how I feel most of the time!!!

Are you starting to understand???

This is how you start to write truly honest lyrics, and this will lead to good things. Trust me. So now do it!!! GO!!!

OK!!!

SO WHAT'S NEXT???

READ ON!!!

The next song…

Should have ONE PHRASE!!!

YES, ONE PHRASE!!!

DO IT!!!

Follow the same steps above but ADD:

1. A bridge (2-4 chords)

2. Write a phrase - at least 3 words - but no more then 7!!!

This is how I did my next song, also on the website (www.chazaray.com), STRIP POKER & THE BIG YELLOW FAN. Here's the phrase I wrote:

Aces blown away...

That's it!!!

Another hit!!!

AWESOME!!!

I used a memory I had of playing strip poker in a room where there was a big yellow fan. Kind of weird, I know... but whatever. Don't judge!!! With this song, I use the title and the lyrics to tell the story. It's a bit hack-poetic but it works.

As you'll hear, I've mostly abandoned my rock style of writing and started messing around with new sounds/beats/etc. BREAKDOWN is a bit alt-pop and STRIP POKER & THE BIG YELLOW FAN has a classical vibe. I love writing music so I really don't care what genre a song ends up being. I just want to write music and lyrics that make sense. There is still some rock influence in all of it, but the progressions are definitely not what I used to do (the verse/verse/chorus stuff). But like I said, I was unable to respectably finish songs using the traditional structure. There's a great expression that says: *'A good plan today is better than a perfect plan tomorrow.'* To me that means I'd rather write a good song today rather than wait for the perfect song tomorrow (because tomorrow never comes).

OK!!!

BACK TO WORK!!!

So now you've done a one word song (your first platinum hit!!!), and you've done a one phrase song (you second hit!!!). Now it's time for your 3rd!!!

For the next song come up with 4 SIMPLE PHRASES. And by simple, I mean REEEAALLLY simple. This is what I did in my song LIGHTS OUT, a dark country tune. The phrases are simple, simple, simple!!! One of them is *'I'm falling.'* Simple, right?!?!? Just make sure the four phrases belong together; make sure they're all related; make sure they all make sense. This is exactly how I wrote this song. Here are the lyrics:

Lights out
I'm falling
I crash down
I'm broken
(Turn on the light!)

Okay, so I added a 5th line, but it doesn't come in until the very end. I did that after listening to the song a bunch of times and started hearing that extra melody. You can do the same. I came up with the lyrics by recalling another old memory about my sister and I having a bunk bed when we were kids. I would sleep on the top bunk and fall off in the middle of the night, crashing down in the floor. Scary, right? Broke my collar bone once. These lyrics are honest. Make sure yours are, too. (By the way, these were the days when there weren't any guard rails. You also didn't have to wear a seatbelt in the car. Anyway…)

You can tell a story or a snippet of your life, just do it with some flair; with some color; with some original vocabulary.

BUT DON'T ANNOUNCE IT!!!!!!!

Just subtly hint at it, ok? Notice I didn't write: *'From on top of my bunk bed.'* That'd be too much information and it'd be completely lame. You never want to tell your audience what to think. NEVER!!! Let them come up with their own visuals. Tell them *just enough*. Even be *somewhat vague*. If you tell the listener what to think, they'll get BORED. For example:

From on top of my bunk bed
I fell down during the night
And crashed down on the floor
And broke my little bones

YAWN!!!!!!!

Did you fall asleep halfway through??? Now do you understand why you shouldn't be too specific??? A great song SPARKS THE LISTENER'S IMAGINATION!!! Too much detail BLOCKS the listeners imagination and turns your song into a boring text book. Keep your words simple and keep them creative.

ALSO!!!

Don't ever use words like *'morning light'* or *'in my mind'* or anything like that. Many writers do (YOU KNOW WHO YOU ARE!!!), but great writers don't. Dig? Keep it original.

SO!!!

You get the idea, right? You're starting to believe, right?!?!?

For this 3rd song, just follow the same steps for the first and second songs.

DO IT NOW!!!

OK!!!

You can think of ONE COOL WORD that has special meaning, can't you?!?!? (Man, I hope so. If not then there's really no hope for you.)

AND!!!

You can come up with ONE COOL PHRASE that has special meaning to you, right???

FINALLY, you can come up with FOUR COOL PHRASES that have special meaning, right???

Please say YES!!!

It REALLY doesn't get easier than that!! (Okay, nothing worthwhile in life is easy, but this is close.)

Right now, because of this method, I can almost manage a verse/verse/chorus song. I'm getting very close but, honestly, at this point I'm beyond grateful that I can write these more simple lyrical songs. They mean a whole lot more to me than some epic rock song with stupid lyrics about irrelevant crap.

OK!!!

SO WHAT'S NEXT???

The next song…

Should have TWO VERSES!!!!!

Don't be frightened!!! Each verse is only 3 SHORT LINES!!!

Just keep it simple. This is what I did in my song SWEET DREAMS. It's just 2 verses, each with 3 lines!!! I used an old expression, *'You made your own bed,'* and went from there. I thought of this lyric because I was pissed off one day and I realized it was all my fault. This old expression came into my head and I started singing it (as I was literally making my bed). So I actually wrote the 1st verse and melody before I even picked up my guitar. Later that day I wrote the 2nd verse (while being mindful of the anger and disappointment that inspired the 1st verse). Here are the lyrics:

You made your own bed
Have a good sleep
Sweetdreams

You knocked yourself out
With one good swing
Sweetdreams

Sweetdreams, my love
Sweetdreams

I vamped the title a little, too, but that's ok. I was just following the music and the melody and that's where it wanted to go. This song got me a bit closer to the traditional verse/verse/chorus structure, so that was nice.

NOW IT'S YOUR TURN!!!

Think of a simple 3-line verse (as you can see my 3rd line is only one word: *'Sweetdreams'*!!!). Then add a second verse that's related.

BE HONEST!!!

Hmmm… how do you be honest???

Get MAD at yourself!!! Why are you mad at yourself?!?!? What'd you do?!?!? What can you do better?!?!? Why are you so AWESOME?!? What's so awesome about you?!?!? Why can't chicks resist you?!?!? Who do you dream of being?!? What's he like?!? Is he a badass?!?!?

Get inspired.

GO!!!

The next song on my website (www.chazaray.com) is WENDELL WISE. This is a melancholy pop song that I managed to write 2 full verses for!!! Yes!!! The lyrics were inspired by a text message to a friend. The text was *'Frisky hermit walking backwards'* and I thought, hmm… that could be a cool song. I squeaked out 6 lines for each verse!!! Awesome!!! Definite progress!!! Below are the lyrics:

Wendell Wise
Frisky hermit walking backwards
Beep, beep, beep
He looks so sad behind those eyes
He dreams about a weekend by the ocean
But finds himself half-sleeping in the dark

Wendell Wise
He wants the girls to love him badly
Please, please, please
He soon decides to buy some time
He sneaks around and looks for more affection
But only sees that everything is gone

The song most resembles the AAA structure, that is; no true chorus. It was out of my control. I was tinkering with a music progression (very, very, very similar to one of my favorite *AC/DC* songs) and the text message about the hermit came into my head and I started singing along. It fit perfectly. I played it over and over again and imagined who this hermit was; what he looked like; how he felt; what he wanted; what he dreamed of; etc, etc, etc… until a complete verse formed. Then I realized it was an AAA-style song. I've learned to never argue, debate, or negotiate with music because it always knows best!!!

So when you're ready, try this approach!!!

Come up with ONE LINE about someone (either real or imaginary) and then write 2 VERSES about them. Each verse should contain 6 LINES. Keep it simple!!!

AAAAAARRGHH!!!!!!!!

KEEP EVERYTHING SIMPLE!!!!!!

The next song on my website is called CONGRESS. It's very much an experimental song. The first thing I came up with was the progression at the end and the accompanying lyrics (which came to me as I was singing along… that's how it happens sometimes, right???). It's a fun bar-room ditty, but I had no ideas for a beginning. Because of the lyrics at the end, I knew the song was about the disturbing behavior of the U.S. government… BUT!!! Notice how the lyrics are not: *'disturbing behavior of the U.S. government'*??? It's merely: *'fighting on the left, fighting on the right.'*

That's what I mean about not telling the audience what to think!!!

Sure, the title of the song implies the government - and in my mind that's what the song is about - but *'fighting on the left, fighting on the right'* can apply to a lot of different scenarios (like my own family!!!). Therefore, the song will mean different things to different people. Remember, don't tell the audience every detail and NEVER tell them what to think!!!

Anyway, after I had the ending of the song, I started searching for a beginning. I was just messing around - just improvising a melody on the low guitar strings while singing along - and I ended up with some experimental free-form weirdo stuff. Since the ending was so tight and predictable, having free-form stuff in the beginning felt right. I came up with the line, *'Don't play with us again,'* and kept it because it fit the theme. I didn't push it and try to write something brilliant (which I can't do anyway). I just kept it simple and somewhat loose. Here are the lyrics:

Oh, why don't you play us again?
Oh, why don't you play us again?
Oh, why don't you sad dickheads?

Oh, why don't you play us again?
Your lies won't save us and take this away
Don't know why you're insane
Don't know why

Hmm, hmm, hmm, hmm

And now there's fighting on the left
And fighting on the right

This song is much different from what I normally do, but I really kind of like it. The lesson here is to not let traditional song structure mess you up!!! Do whatever you want. There are no rules. If you come up with a cool 2-chord ditty, then go with it!!! Just make it original and make it your own. Always make it your own!!!

AND HEY!!!!!!

You don't have to change the world with one song!!! Write a few lines about your car and let the audience figure out the brilliant metaphors and deeper meanings and all that stuff. Just keep it simple, simple, simple!!!

OK!!!!

SO THAT'S IT!!!

That's the NEW PLAN!!!

BUT WAIT!!!!

There's ONE FINAL TASK!!!!!

READ ON!!!

Once you've completed the above songs - and you'll be fired up if you do, believe me!!! But once you do, you'll be ready to expand your lyrical abilities. Here's what I want you to do:

Go back to the 1st task - the ONE WORD song - and do it again. Come up with another song with another word… BUT!!!! This time add some phrases that relate to the one word. Use your stream of conscious and sing along. Make stuff up. Don't worry about how silly it is, just do it and write it all down. If I did this with my song BREAKDOWN, some phrases I might add are:

Breakdown
On the rush hour train

Bruising my brain
She won't stop calling
I keep dreaming I'm awake
Getting pushed around
Losing control of it all

SEE WHAT I DID???

'*Breakdown*' is the theme and I came up with stuff that's directly related. No need to worry about rhyming or the phrases relating to *each other* - but they DO have to relate to '*Breakdown*.'

That's it!!! That's how you start to expand your writing!!!

NEXT!!!!

In my song LIGHTS OUT there are 4 phrases (ok, there's actually 5) and they are all related to *each other*.

Lights out
I'm falling
I crash down
I'm broken
(Turn on the light!)

Using the same strategy, go back to the 3rd task - the 4 PHRASES song - and do it again... BUT!!!! This time come up with 12 PHRASES that are all connected to *each other*... as if you're telling a story. If you're feeling lucky, then expand it to 24!!! It'll be your defining moment as a songwriter!!!

If I expanded LIGHTS OUT, here's how it might

happen (sticking with the original THEME and using that 5th line as a refrain):

Lights out
I'm falling
I crash down
I'm broken
(Turn on the light!)

I cry out
And pass out
Lying there
In darkness
(Turn on the light!)

Alone now
Reaching out
With cold hands
To no one
(Turn on the light!)

OK!!!

Do you UNDERSTAND?!?!?!?

Again…

THIS IS HOW YOU EXPAND YOUR ABILITY!!!

Now…

TWO CRUCIALLY IMPORTANT POINTS TO ALWAYS REMEMBER!!!

In the expanded version of LIGHT'S OUT one of the phrases is, *'With cold hands.'* However, in an earlier draft of this book I had written, *'With helpless hands.'*

So why did I change it?!?!?

A very important point I made earlier applies to this!!! Don't tell the audience what to think and don't tell them every detail. By using the word *'cold'* I've made the line very open to the audience's interpretation yet still maintaining the nature of the original line.

AND!!!!!

The word *'helpless'* is way too OBVIOUS, DRAMATIC, LAME, etc… AND it sounds WEAK and it's a definite buzz kill. Don't be a BUZZ KILL!!! Audiences don't like weak songwriters. Neither do you. In fact, there aren't any who are successful!!! You can still write about your faults, fears, complaints and weaknesses. Just do it without being a whining, wussy, 'poor me' crybaby.

BE CONFIDENT NO MATTER WHAT!!!

OK!!!!!

You know what?

I'M SO AWESOME…

HERE!!! I'M GOING TO GIVE YOU A SONG!!!

It's called, *'THINGS I LIKE'*

Things I like
Sushi on Tuesday
A good night's sleep
A girl smiling at me
Drinks with buds
The midtown buzz
The river at dusk
Wearing a coat
Playing in snow

BOOM!!!

The song kind of stinks, I know!! (Disclaimer: I just typed this in realtime, so whatever.) But it actually doesn't suck too bad because the lyrics make sense. I'm just trying to make a point here. But, heck, use the song!! Put a couple chords to it!!! Enjoy!!!

OK!!!

HEY, YOU!!!

GET BUSY!!!

If you try out all of the above, you'll start to figure out what kind of lyricist you are. We often get stuck with crappy lyrics or a lack of *any* lyrics because we don't know what to write about or we don't know what to say... BUT!!! This will change once you find your comfort zone - and the way to find your comfort zone is to start small. You'll start to figure out what themes are closest to your heart; what your spirit and soul naturally want to say.

This is important!!!

Your confidence will grow as a writer and you'll be able to get more accomplished. If you sing your own songs, then you'll start to sing better and more confidently and, believe me, people will notice. Starting small will help you not waste words and help you keep everything nice and tight. When you feel ready to expand to a larger song then you'll have a good idea of how to do it and how to keep it just as tight.

Remember, if you can't do it small then you can't do it big.

OK!!!

So once you get the hang of writing honest lyrics, the next step is to make them ULTRA COOL. If you write with confidence and you're not a buzz kill then you'll be halfway there… BUT!!! To get your lyrics *all* the way there, there's one more thing you have to do: Imagine millions of people singing them.

We all sing our favorite songs. Right now I could sing hundreds of songs from the Beatles, Led Zeppelin, Radiohead, Johnny Cash, Eric B. & Rakim, Elton John, Stevie Wonder, Taj Mahal, Lorde, and who knows how many others. Sure, I don't know all the lyrics… BUT!!! I know enough.

And that's the goal.

People won't sing lame lyrics. They're not going to sing, '*with helpless hands.*' Hell, they're not even going to sing, '*with cold hands*!' The latter lyric is a good start, though, because it's honest - but now I have to push that lyric through the *'cool'* filter. If I can't… well, that'd be okay, too. Not *every line* has to be worthy of a million singers, but you should at least try to get them all there.

Finally, while you're making your lyrics more cool and singable, you should also be making your melodies as strong as possible. Like with your lyrics, your melody shouldn't be a buzz kill. No one likes a mumbling, fumbling, boring melody. Make it interesting right from the start. Your melody should also have ENERGY. It doesn't have to be high-octane… BUT!!! There has to be something!!! And while you're at it, give your melody an interesting RHYTHM, too. Make it unique. Make it you. Make it awesome!!! If you want people to sing your song, then give them a song worth singing.

Listen to some pop songs (or any great song); listen to the dynamics of the melody, to the rhythm of the singing, to the energy of the voice!!! It's really not that complicated.

Perhaps the most powerful thing about music is that it provides an escape for the listener. For three minutes, the listener can get lost in a song and forget about their problems. Music can turn bad times into good times, and it can turn good times into great times. So try not to mess with people's escape. People don't want to go to a depressing, boring, preachy place. They want to get fired-up and sing!!!

OK!!!

One last suggestion is to find a writing partner, or at least a songwriting critic. Not your mom!!! Someone who writes better than you (or has a great ear for music). This can be very, very beneficial and help you grow as a writer. I don't have a songwriting partner but wish I did. Someone like Paul McCartney would be cool.

That was a joke.

But not really.

AND DON'T FORGET!!!

If you think of a good phrase (or word!!) or hear someone say one, then WRITE IT DOWN!! You never know when you can use it and/or combine it with other phrases. Pretty soon you'll have a whole supply to work with!!!

OK!!!!!

Anyone can write great meaningful lyrics and I hope the above approach helps you out and gets you going in the right direction. Just go slow. Don't try to do too much. Keep it simple and keep it honest. That's all you've got to do. Okay???

OK!!!!!

BUT WAIT!!!

WHAT ABOUT MUSIC!?!?!?

I haven't brought up MUSIC yet so I'd like to add some thoughts about that.

Keeping music simple is the best way for me to

write songs. There's nothing wrong with using C/F/G!!! (And then maybe an A Minor!!!) But... I always try to find unique ways to play them.

THAT'S THE KEY!!!

C/F/G has been played over and over again for centuries so you have to make it your own. I usually use fragmented chords (I don't even know what they are until later). When you're writing, try to be as original as possible without being difficult and complicated. Don't have 27 parts to your song. That's just stupid. If you can't write a great song with 3 chords then stop writing music. The best songs of ALL TIME only have a few chords.

Think about it.

In my song BREAKDOWN the main riff is C to A Minor. Simple, right? But... the chords are being played in a unique way: I'm finger-picking them and playing a melody at the same time (kind of). Listen to it. When the singing starts I add another chord: F Major 7. That might sound fancy but all I'm doing is playing a standard F chord and leaving the high E string open. As you already know, when you play a progression long enough, you start fiddling with chords and end up with stuff like that. Anyway, BREAKDOWN has only 3 chords.

I used to know a guy who was awesome at guitar and had a great voice and was a real pro. I believe he could've been a successful recording artist. In fact, I have no doubt... BUT!!! His first self-released album was an absolute bore. All his songs - and I mean ALL OF THEM - had so many parts, so many chords, so many changes that, as a listener, I couldn't keep up and worst of all, I couldn't connect. That's what I mean about not having 27 parts to your song. Keep it simple. If you can't do it simple, then you sure as hell can't do it complex.

Another good rule to follow (most of the time) is to keep your songs as short as possible. Don't have a minute-long intro or a three minute solo or an extra verse. No one wants to hear it. Believe me. And neither will you (a year from now). Ask yourself if every moment in your song is necessary. If not, then take it out. Get to the singing quickly and get to the hook quickly. Try listening to some Mozart… talk about not wasting any time. His compositions are tight and compact!!! Make sure yours are, too.

OK!!!!!

THAT'S IT!!!

REALLY!!!

UGH!!!

That's the best I can do.

I really, really, really hope the info here helps you out. I wish I'd known this stuff a long time ago. If you found it useful (or life-changing!!!) and enjoyed some of my songs, please consider buying one!!! That'd be awesome and so much appreciated. The website is www.chazaray.com.

OK!!!

THAT'S IT!!!

This is the end!!

Now get out there and CONQUER!!!!!!!

I wish you all the BEST OF LUCK!!!

But more importantly…

Have some fun,
chazaray

(One final note… I apologize for all the capital letters and exclamation points. I hardly ever write like this. In fact, I never do. That's not me. Really. I just got fired-up for some reason. I couldn't help it. Maybe I should talk to someone.)

About the author:
Friendly, cool, and mildly psychotic. Lives in New York City.

www.chazaray.com